STRYKERS

BY DENNY VON FINN

EPIC

BELLWETHER MEDIA · MINNEAPOLIS, MN

EPIC BOOKS are no ordinary books. They burst with intense action, high-speed heroics, and shadows of the unknown. Are you ready for an Epic adventure?

This edition first published in 2014 by Bellwether Media, Inc.

No part of this publication may be reproduced in whole or in part without written permission of the publisher. For information regarding permission, write to Bellwether Media, Inc., Attention: Permissions Department, 5357 Penn Avenue South, Minneapolis, MN 55419.

Library of Congress Cataloging-in-Publication Data

Von Finn, Denny.
   Strykers / by Denny Von Finn.
      pages cm. – (Epic: Military vehicles)
   Includes bibliographical references and index.
   Summary: "Engaging images accompany information about Strykers. The combination of high-interest subject matter and light text is intended for students in grades 2 through 7"– Provided by publisher.
   Audience: Grades 2-7.
   ISBN 978-1-62617-082-7 (hardcover : alk. paper)
   1. Stryker armored vehicle–Juvenile literature. I. Title.
   UG446.5.V623 2014
   623.74'75–dc23
                        2013035939

Printed in the United States of America, North Mankato, MN.

The photographs in this book are reproduced through the courtesy of the United States Department of Defense.
A special thanks to the following for additional photos: Kim Jae Hwan / Newscom, front cover, p. 21; Mark Fitz / Alamy

TABLE OF CONTENTS

STRYKERS

The city bakes in the desert sun. Enemy soldiers hide in old buildings. Suddenly, there is a loud rumble outside. Strykers are bringing U.S. soldiers to fight the enemy!

Enemy bullets bounce off the Strykers. A **gunner** in each Stryker returns fire.

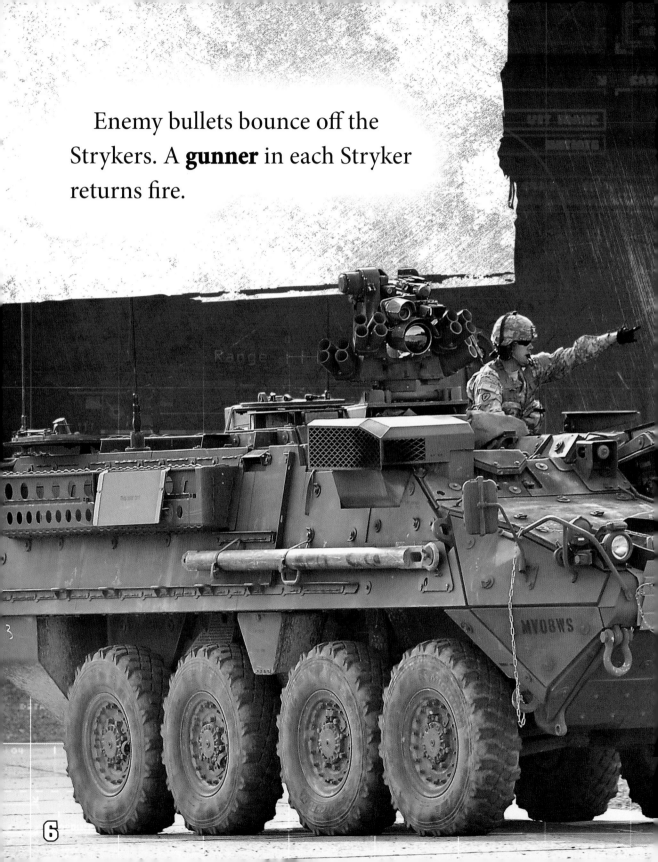

GUNNER

Stryker Fact

The U.S. Army has more than 4,000 Strykers in service.

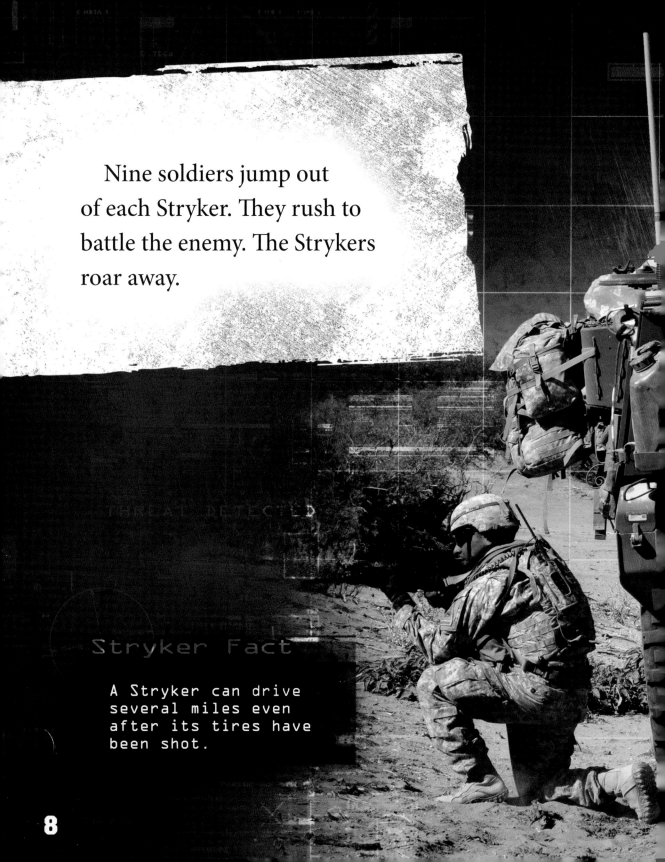

Nine soldiers jump out of each Stryker. They rush to battle the enemy. The Strykers roar away.

Stryker Fact

A Stryker can drive several miles even after its tires have been shot.

A-21

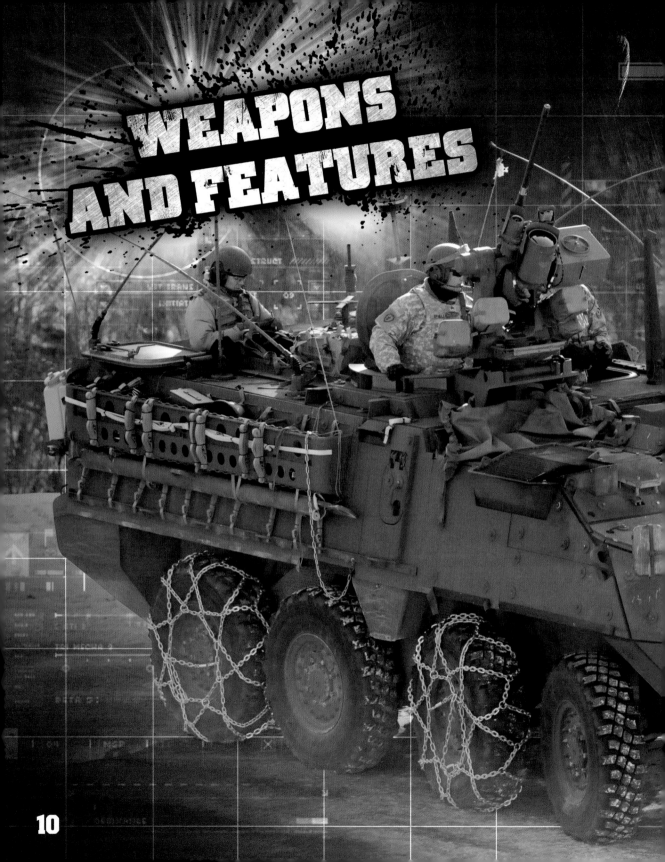

WEAPONS AND FEATURES

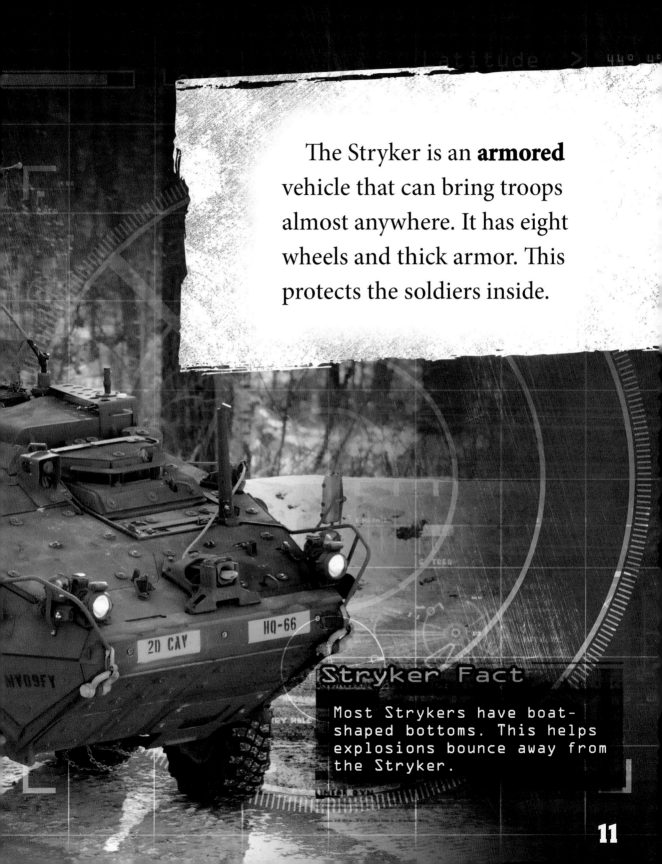

The Stryker is an **armored** vehicle that can bring troops almost anywhere. It has eight wheels and thick armor. This protects the soldiers inside.

Stryker Fact

Most Strykers have boat-shaped bottoms. This helps explosions bounce away from the Stryker.

Most Strykers have a **grenade launcher** and a **machine gun**. A gunner can use a **periscope** to shoot these weapons from inside the Stryker.

GRENADE
LAUNCHER

MACHINE
GUN

MORTAR

Other Strykers carry **missiles**. They are used to destroy enemy tanks. Some Strykers also fire **mortars**. They support U.S. soldiers on the ground.

MISSILE LAUNCHER

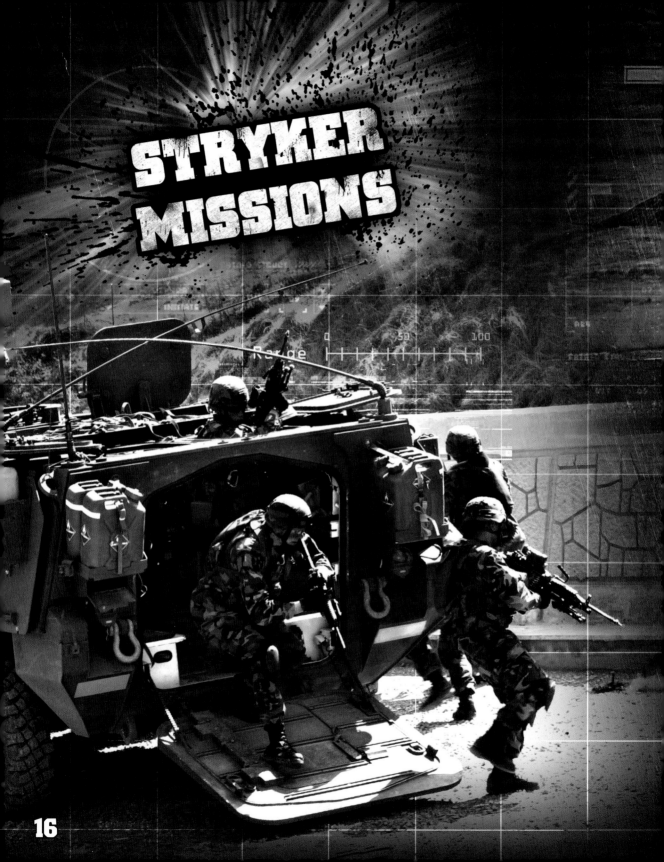

STRYKER MISSIONS

Stryker **missions** take the vehicles over all types of land. They can move quickly and are always ready for battle. This has made them important vehicles in the **War on Terror**.

Strykers carry troops to battle and perform **recon** missions. Some Strykers destroy **IEDs** hidden by the enemy. Others serve as ambulances.

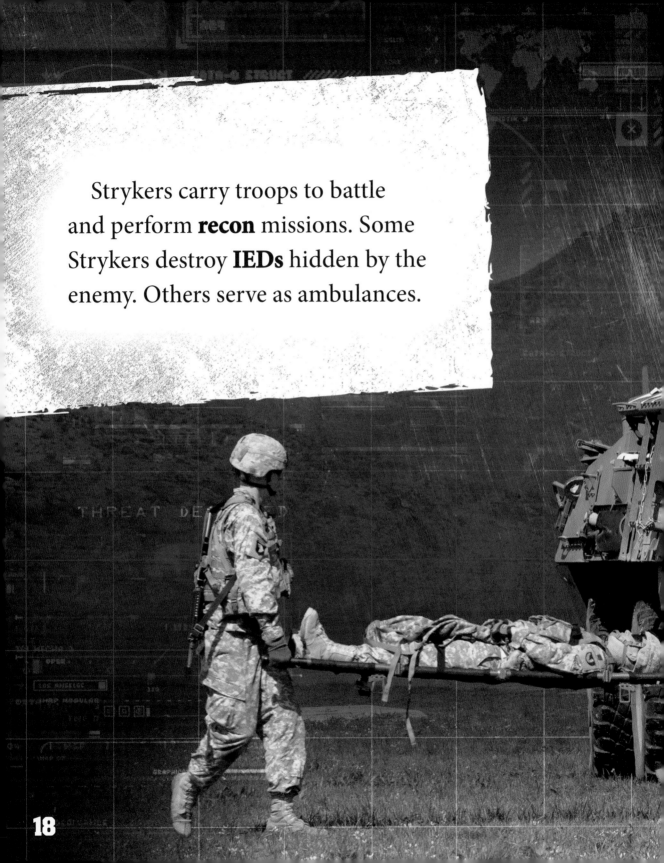

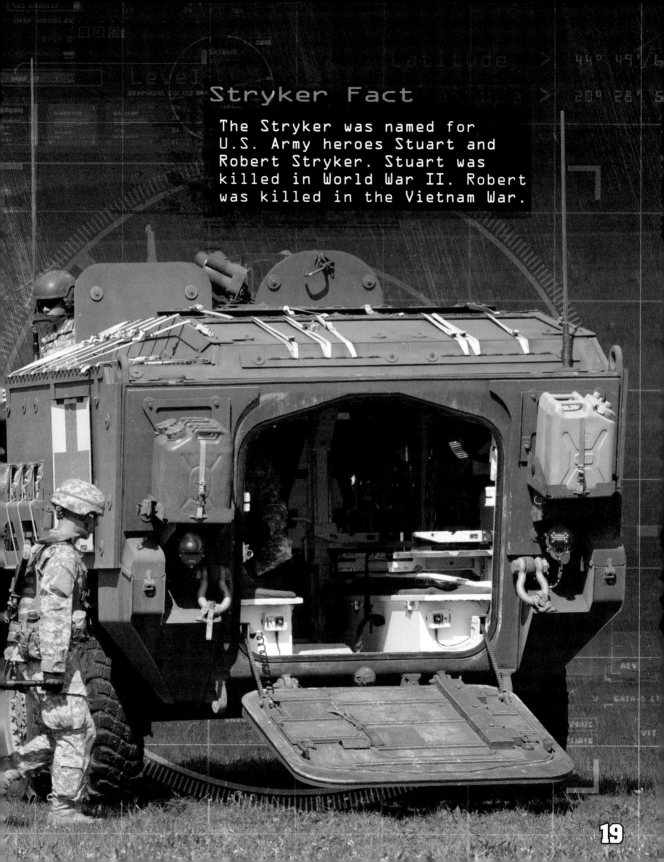

Stryker Fact

The Stryker was named for U.S. Army heroes Stuart and Robert Stryker. Stuart was killed in World War II. Robert was killed in the Vietnam War.

VEHICLE BREAKDOWN: STRYKER

Used By:	**U.S. Army**
Entered Service:	**2002**
Length:	**22 feet, 11 inches (7 meters)**
Height:	**8 feet, 8 inches (2.6 meters)**
Vehicle Weight:	**38,000 pounds (17,237 kilograms)**
Top Speed:	**60 miles (97 kilometers) per hour**
Range:	**330 miles (531 kilometers)**
Crew:	**2 or more**
Weapons:	**machine gun, grenade launcher, missiles, or mortars**
Missions:	**troop transport, firepower, recon, medical aid**

Strykers keep soldiers safe and enemies on the run. They can do anything the Army needs them to do!

GLOSSARY

armored—covered with thick steel and ceramic plates to protect from enemy fire

grenade launcher—a weapon that fires small explosives called grenades

gunner—the Stryker crew member who searches for targets and fires the vehicle's weapons

IEDs—homemade but very deadly bombs; IED stands for "improvised explosive device."

machine gun—a weapon that fires bullets rapidly

missiles—explosives that are guided to a target

missions—military tasks

mortars—weapons that launch small explosives great distances

periscope—a telescope-like device that sticks out of the top of the Stryker; gunners use periscopes to see their surroundings.

recon—a mission that involves gathering information about the enemy

War on Terror—a war led by the United States to stop organized groups from performing acts of violence; the War on Terror began in 2001.

TO LEARN MORE

At the Library

Alvarez, Carlos. *Strykers*. Minneapolis, Minn.: Bellwether Media, 2011.

Hamilton, John. *Strykers*. Minneapolis, Minn.: ABDO Pub. Co., 2012.

Shank, Carol. *U.S. Military Assault Vehicles*. North Mankato, Minn.: Capstone Press, 2013.

On the Web

Learning more about Strykers is as easy as 1, 2, 3.

1. Go to www.factsurfer.com.

2. Enter "Strykers" into the search box.

3. Click the "Surf" button and you will see a list of related Web sites.

With factsurfer.com, finding more information is just a click away.

INDEX